For me, on my 30th birthday.

"The creative adult is the child who has survived."
-Ursula K. Le Guin

Contents

Imagination Mussels
Across Lake Erie I look
for Africa. I am told that zebras are invading

the beaches. It is why we wade in
with water shoes. I am young

and feel the coarse manes
brush against my calves and feel the skulls

crack under my rubber soles. I could scream
but my grandfather is fishing for quiet

from the boulders. He says children
are better seen than heard, my mind

tearing open on unicorn horns,
fusing together again like a muscle.

All Is Better With Butter
Maybe time
is like a kernel
wedged against
the baby tooth
that still survives
30 years later
in the bottom row.
I try not to think
too much of it,
whether I am
the popcorn
or the molar -
whether life likes
to linger near me
or if it is slowly
sinking away.

A List Of Things You Shouldn't Pickle
You shouldn't shove dread into a jar
and drown it with dill seeds and vinegar. You

used to hold your breath driving past cemeteries,
never met the smell of mint leaf and bergamot.

You tried to brine anger, set it out
in the sun and soften the reaction.

The longer you take to admitting that
you are the one who spilled the marinade, the madder

he gets. And you once bit too soon into a problem
thinking it was a pickle, but it was still

too cucumber crisp, and then you realized
love shouldn't take this long to relish.

Choked Up

Even after all that time - even after
    the years and the arthritic hands
and the final verse swelled,
    she saved him. She might have
scalpelled his throat with a pick, offered
    the neck of a ukulele, but
she sang his airways apart, compressed
    a symphony from his lungs,
and how could she have known
    it was the sound that kept him
        from breathing?

"You Said You Weren't Afraid To Die"
                    -Bright Eyes

It's sort of ironic
        the way he colors me Canary.

I sat here long after
        the sentinels -

I let them convince me
        it was safe.

Will it take long?
        No.

Do you regret it?
        No.

Does it hurt?
        Only a little.

I ask them through the shading
        and the agony,

Are the birds better off brave
        or oblivious?

.08

I know so little
    of many things - that
the fuel needs stabilizer
    before mowing or else
the carburetor clogs
    and then the quack grass
and the ragweed
    and the clover
patches like a pair
    of old jeans. Who knew,
at 30, high school's denim
    could still button
at the waist, and that
    a high school friend
could still be a friend,
    and that sisters grow best
in sangria soil - never cut
    off whether she says too
much or nothing at all.

Grow Up

He says the way that I peel my finger nails like potatoes
says something about me. There

is a confetti of Essie Lady Like and Clothing
Optional in the couch cushions. It says that

I like a party but I don't like the clean up. And Christmas
lights up before November apparently says

something about my patience, but who else
can see a picture of it and not need their tree nailed to the ceiling

immediately? He should really be impressed
that the frames on our shelves are no longer filled

with the family portraits that came with them, and that
I no longer sleep with the silk of a blankie

weaved between my fingers. And he should never tell me to
grow up. I mean, just look at those lawn lines.

Needs An Island In The Kitchen
When you ate the penny
you first sucked it's copper
tang. You flipped it head to tail
to head to your belly.
What inside of you is so starved?
You have honey goat cheese
in the refrigerator, rotting
cucumber in the crisper drawer.
A penny is a penny until you chew it
thirty times, and then
a penny is just an idea they had.
A penny, a penny, a penny.
A penny is just a sound made
by lips, teeth, and tongue.

<u>The Tile Setter Had A Daughter</u>
In her first home,
in the disemboweled
bathroom, he taught her
the consistency
of mortar. She had
walked on it
all of her life, on
the places where he had
taken to his knees, grouted
his joints, leveled
the ground beneath her.
If you add too much water
it will lose it's grit.
When she was a child
she begged for a floor
of steel springs.
If you don't add enough
it will not bond.
He stretched his resilience
in buoyant black canvas,
tested the rungs
under his weight. *Leave*
space so that it can
expand. She jumped
into spreading the trowel -
giggled as they played
in the mud.

<u>The Floor Was Never Lava</u>
and the world was never
      some Disney Land, just
            as the stars were never
your wishes or your dead
      grandmother or some place
            you'll ever reach. Adulthood
is spinning in tiny tea cups,
      swallowing reality down, trying
            not to hurl it into the laps
      of our children.

As The Waitstaff Sings Happy Birthday
I gripe, laugh nervously, hide
behind red delicious cheeks. Thirty
candles drip pink, waxy tears
onto dessert. *Make a wish,* they say.
I wish in consolation. I wish
for the man beside me to stop staring,
for cinnamon apples on the cheesecake.
At a booth in back a baby cries. Wishing
for life would be fruitless. An apple tree
requires chilled winters to set bloom,
and still there are so many warm women
wishing. How about a pair of jeans
that don't sag in the knees, to find
the diamond that I lost from my wedding
ring, for just one good night's sleep?
I close my eyes, take in a breath, wish
for fuzzy socks in the gift bags, and
for a snow day that shuts down the city.

Crow's Feet

Each year we host a murder
        in our kitchen. The drawer
beside the oven hardly shuts
        anymore. A roost of dead
batteries, spools of needle-
        stabbed thread, carcasses
of used up red pens. They hunger.
        They speculate
on my belly - on my stow
        of the croze, and when
they leave they latch
        their talons to our temples - tell us
that we are not getting any
        younger. I want to tell them that
each night I elevate my hips, but
        we can't all be conquerors of gravity.

Leaves Of Three

First, my feet itched
and then the arches inflated
                with pink, fleshy balloons.
I could have floated away
    by my ankles, but then
this is what happens
                when we stand too long
in places we shouldn't. Remember
    when I asked you
what poison ivy looks like?
                It looks like 5:50AM, hazelnut
creamer with a splash of coffee,
    butterscotch dog hair
stuck to black pants.

Pareidolia
I imagine time to a dog
must be peanut butter
spread across stale bread.

And to the dog I spread
like strawberry jelly
across Sunnyside Drive?

All I can be sure of
is that I can no longer eat
my toast dipped in yolk.

That Will Leave A Scar
Dehydrated strawberries
soak in the diffuser

after bleeding all over
the kitchen sink,

and the cupboards, and the doors,
and the carpeting.

The dog remains a callous,
the couch a grabby hand,

and all is sticky
as honey.

"Poets Have Been Mysteriously Silent On The Subject Of Cheese"
-G.K. Chesterton

You may not hear their snoring, yet
        there are at least 30,000
stink bugs asleep in the walls. Every
        now and then the whiff
of cilantro, silent cleansers of my taste
        buds, and now I can no longer eat

Chipotle white rice. Your mother was
        never one to wash your mouth out
with soap, though you enjoy the taste of it
        every now and then. And the horrible things
you do to cheese, stuffing it in mushroom
        caps, topping the tilapia. I could guess

you're the type to slip your socks on
        with sandals and welcome winter
in white. But I will keep to my brown
        marmorated sweaters, block cheddar
without the parade, the quiet and simplicity
        inside these snug walls.

Polar Vortex Of 2015
The trees bare all
but bones, waiting
for the sky to drop
it's blanket. I am
in my bed, and you
in yours, but we are both
soon beneath the same
one hundred and fifty nine
miles of white. We are
men and women
of snow, smuggling
pines into our homes -
into our chests,
and when we are apart
the brightness of my heart
is a tree with lights
strung by you.

Presbyopia

She has started to hold me further away.
        She says that she can't see me anymore
                when I am under her nose.

She places me down on my feet, asks me
        to keep walking. I have always
                minded my mother, and so I take my first steps

across the living room. I walk across the field to school,
        to the other side of Michigan, to a man
                at the end of an aisle. I go

until the birth cord breaks, until I forget
        that we were ever even attached. *There*
                you are, she says. *I can see you now.*

Paper Trails

We watch the seals swim in the harbour
  of a village you will never see, famished
starlings stick their beaks into our battered
          cod. I wish you could smell the barley, sweet
and bitter, sipped in a city where stories are
  poured perfectly past the brim - in a country
that once emptied its belly into our homes, roots
          stretched from Royal Road to Whitaker.
I worry that one day the next of us will
  never walk Windover, and so I leave words
behind, breadcrumbs, leading to my front door.

The Sweetest Morning

when oranges undressed
to champagne flutes - toasts
and marmalade. Savory
the evening when we danced
until the wine dried
and our heels were pressed
to their piths.

London Before Children

Families flood the Southbank.
The night muddies rain.

And your cider, bee broth,
is full of sun. Drink it.

I will take down the scaffolding.
I will lift up the bridge

as the guards' eyes flicker
like lightning. They dream

of their babies crowning.
I count the seconds to thunder.

A Visit To Amsterdam

We had planned to see the tulips
on Sunday, but then you opened the curtain,
the buildings lurching back and forth
over the canal. The rain washed away all
of our photographs. We wanted so badly
this day to bloom. Instead, we took shelter
in a river boat. We floated in silence,
just the droplets drumming the glass
ceiling. We listened as if the song spoke
the rebuttal to how barren soil could suddenly
blossom, rebel nature without reason,
decide red lights mean go.

Endometrium Is Unremarkable
One night
the North Star fell
and the Little Dipper
lost it's handle.
The night had nothing
left to hold onto -
nothing to ladle
up the darkness
and light up the bathroom
at 2AM. But then,
there it was, the second
star to the right
that led us straight on
to the morning switch -
to mom's chicken
noodle soup,
and to when she said,
One day, you will be
remarkable.

<u>Motherly</u>
My little sister bends her neck
to me, which is to say
that she concedes.

What is it to be first-born,
if not taller, then
to be mildly uppish, just enough

to gain an extra few inches
in stature? Which is to say that I am struggling
to keep my head above the hot air

balloons. And here I am, grounded
for an entire month
for pushing my little sister

onto the floor. I am forced
to weave baskets with my mother,
which is to say that I am becoming the basket

weaver rather than the groundee,
which is to say that I am helping
raise beauty into the sky.

<u>My Husband Is On A 24 Foot Ladder</u>
flashing the side of the chimney,

my sister is waiting
for a heartbeat,

and I am in the kitchen thawing
chicken in the sink.

I scrub the salmonella
out from under my fingernails

before placing contact lenses
onto my eyes, and somehow

it makes me see
the slip-and-slide at Camp Willi Wise,

the blue tarp like keratitis
scraping against my bare thighs,

and sucking my belly in
beneath a one piece

bathing suit. And here I am, still
afraid to wear a bikini -

here I am, still thawing
in the kitchen sink

as my sister waits
for a heartbeat.

Ode To The Hideout

You were a thawing pool, early
spring, a wrought iron chair that survived

thirteen winters without rust. The whistle
of the early robin from the birch

bones. We were mud in the living room -
mouths that nearly surrendered shut. We thought

there was nowhere left to hide, and then you
drip fed us berries as the ghosts barrelled

like bitter porter. You were the pellets
for thoughts. You left us
open.

A Lesson On Appreciation
Ninth mile in, I remember that
I have not eaten. The black flies nibbling
at my shins remind me of the beef
sticks in my backpack. We feast, the flies
and I, on salty meat until we remember
                    our thirst.

If the days were dollars, I would spend
them all on inner tubes, and we would
float the lazy rivers and laugh together,
the flies and I, drunk on freshwater,
and we would drift until we remember
                    our hunger.

Where Hope Is

Where the river has just iced over
but still splits under a stumble.

      Where the hearts stop pumping
      and the blood freezes in our veins.

            And where there, at the kindling
            he teaches me with flint to make fire.

<u>Dear Santa</u>
Thank you for the snowfall
of memory on their faces.
There - the slow unwrapping
of morning eyes, the rise
of syrupy grins.

Few dawns are this delicious.
As a child I once debated
God of your existence.
I haven't stopped,
sincerely.

P.S. When you left
the world piled their dishes
back into the sink, brought
their trash bins back
out to the curb.

Until next year?

Raise The Rubaeus
Should time return
in my burned toast
may he be
a happy ghost
and may we learn to love
what isn't
even when it's not
so pleasant
like Monday coffee
cold, bare feet
popcorn pieces
in our teeth
standing in
the two week wait
every lawn line
on her face
the lava
underneath the rug
the hungry, thirsty,
smelly bugs
the growing old
but staying young
because time rewinds
when having fun.

First printing, 2020.

ISBN 978-1-79488-673-5

ISBN 978-1-79488-673-5   90000

9 781794 886735